CONTENTS

Any words appearing in the text in bold, **like this**, are explained in the glossary. You can also look out for them in the Word Bank box at the bottom of each page.

Leonard Lommel and the rest of his US **battalion** fell silent. Their boat was about to land at a beach in Normandy, France.

The task ahead

Their task was to destroy the large enemy guns at the top of the steep cliffs. If they failed, the German soldiers would use the guns. They would use them to kill the American troops arriving on the beach below.

What led to war?

World War I ended in 1918. Germany lost some of its lands and power. In 1933, the Nazi party came to power in Germany. Adolf Hitler (below) was its leader. His attempt to regain these lands led to a second world war.

It is the sixth year of World War II. US troops arrive at a beach in Normandy, France, on 6 June, 1944. They are part of a massive **invasion** by the **Allies**. This invasion day is known as D-Day. D-Day was a key date in World War II.

Word Bank battalion large military unit made up of 200 to 1,000 troops

On the Front Line

UNDER FIRE IN WORLD WAR II

Brian Fitzgerald

www.raintreepublishers.co.uk
Visit our website to find out more information about **Raintree** books.

To order:

 Phone 44 (0) 1865 888113

Send a fax to 44 (0) 1865 314091

 Visit the Raintree Bookshop at **www.raintreepublishers.co.uk** to browse our catalogue and order online.

First published in Great Britain by Raintree,
Halley Court, Jordan Hill, Oxford OX2 8EJ,
part of Harcourt Education.
Raintree is a registered trademark of
Harcourt Education Ltd.

Produced for Raintree Publishers by Discovery Books Ltd
Editorial: Kathryn Walker, Juliet Smith, and Daniel Nunn
Design: Rob Norridge, Michelle Lisseter, and Clare Nicholas
Expert reader: David Downing
Picture research: Amy Sparks
Project manager: Juliet Smith
Production: Duncan Gilbert
Printed and bound in China by South China Printing Company Ltd
Originated by Dot Gradations Ltd

ISBN 1 406 20246 0 (hardback)
10 09 08 07 06
10 9 8 7 6 5 4 3 2 1

ISBN 1 406 20253 3 (paperback)
10 09 08 07 06
10 9 8 7 6 5 4 3 2 1

British Library Cataloguing in Publication Data
Fitzgerald, Brian
  Under Fire in World War II. – Differentiated ed. –
(Freestyle express. On the front line)
1. World War, 1939–1945 – Juvenile literature
I. Title
940.5'4
A full catalogue record for this book is available from the British Library.

This levelled text is a version of *Freestyle: On the Front Line: Under Fire in World War II*

Original edition produced by White-Thomson Publishing Ltd, Bridgewater Business Centre, 210 High Street, Lewes BN7 2NH.

Acknowledgements
The publishers would like to thank the following for permission to reproduce photographs:
AKG pp. 4–5, 6, 9, 12(r), 14, 15, 17, 23, 26(l), 31, 34(r), 36(l), 36–37, 41(l), 41(r); Corbis pp. 8, 12(l), 18–19, 20, 22, 24, 25, 29, 30, 32, 33, 34(l), 35, 38, 40; Harcourt pp. 4(l), 18(l), 39; Popperfoto pp. 10, 11, 27; Topfoto pp. **title page**, 13, 16, 19(r), 21, 26(r), 28.

Cover photograph of US troops landing on a Normandy beach in France on 6 June 1944 reproduced with kind permission of Corbis.

Maps on pp. 7, 22 by Peter Bull.

Source notes: p. 8 Fowler's account taken from *Many Kinds of Courage: An Oral History of World War II* by Richard Lidz; p. 14 Number of ships sunk taken from *Official History*; *War at Sea* vol. 1–3, published in *Battle of the Atlantic* by Terry Hughes and John Costello; pp. 28–29 The account of Vassili Zaitsev's exploits is taken from his autobiography *Notes of a Sniper*; pp. 34–35 Main text: *Band of Brothers* by Stephen Ambrose.

Bravery and success

Lommel left his boat and was immediately hit by a bullet. He was in great pain, but ran until he reached the cliffs. German soldiers shot at him as he climbed upward.

At the top of the cliffs, Lommel found the five large guns. These guns were called **howitzers**. He destroyed them with explosives. Lommel and his battalion had been successful. But the cost was great. More than half of the 225 soldiers in the battalion were either dead or badly injured.

Find out later

What happened at Stalingrad?

Where were these US soldiers captured?

What were these shelters called?

Allies group of nations that fought against Germany, Italy, and Japan in World War II

BLITZKRIEG!

On 1 September 1939, Germany invaded Poland. The Germans used tanks and **dive-bombers** to attack their neighbour. They called this type of warfare "blitzkrieg". Blitzkrieg means "Lightning War", because the attacks were very fast.

World War II begins

Britain and France had promised to help Poland if it was attacked by Germany. Both countries declared war on Germany. World War II had begun.

As the war progressed, other countries also declared war on Germany. These countries that fought the Germans together were called the **Allies**.

World War II timeline

1 September 1939
Germany invades Poland.

9 April 1940
Germany invades Denmark and Norway.

10–13 May 1940
Germany invades Luxembourg, Belgium, the Netherlands, and France.

22 June 1940
France **surrenders** to the Germans.

German soldiers at the Polish border take a rest by a **howitzer**.

Word Bank   dive-bomber plane that dives down towards its target before dropping its explosives

The German advance continues

There was no fighting in the next few months. Both sides prepared for the next stage of the war.

Then, in April 1940, Germany invaded Denmark and Norway. In May 1940, Germany invaded Luxembourg, Belgium, and the Netherlands (also known as Holland). The fast-moving German army then began to invade France.

Winston Churchill
On 10 May 1940, Winston Churchill became Prime Minister of Great Britain. He remained Prime Minister throughout World War II.

This map shows the borders of Europe before World War II began.

NORWAY
SWEDEN
ESTONIA
North Sea
Baltic Sea
LATVIA
DENMARK
LITHUANIA
IRELAND
EAST PRUSSIA
GREAT BRITAIN
NETHERLANDS
Berlin
POLAND
SOVIET UNION
(also known as the USSR)
Dunkirk
BELGIUM
GERMANY
LUXEMBOURG
ATLANTIC
CZECHOSLOVAKIA
OCEAN
FRANCE
SWITZERLAND
AUSTRIA
HUNGARY
ROMANIA
Black Sea
YUGOSLAVIA
BULGARIA
PORTUGAL
ITALY
Adriatic Sea
SPAIN
ALBANIA
TURKEY
GREECE
Mediterranean Sea

N
W E
S

0   500 km
0   300 miles

_ _ _ _ Borders of Europe in the lead
up to World War II

surrender give yourself up to the enemy

Dunkirk

Most of northern France was soon in the hands of the Germans. British troops in France had to either escape or be destroyed.

On the evening of 1 June 1940, Sergeant John Fowler joined other British soldiers. The men were marching to the beach at Dunkirk in France. All kinds of boats had sailed across the **English Channel** to Dunkirk. They came to help the soldiers escape. These boats included military ships, fishing boats, and motorboats.

Miracle at Dunkirk

Dunkirk was a defeat for the Western **Allies** (Britain and France). In a way it was also a success for them. In nine days, more than 338,000 **Allied** troops were rescued. Unfortunately, they had to leave their **ammunition** and vehicles behind.

Hundreds of trapped British and French troops wait to be rescued from the beach at Dunkirk.

Word Bank   ammunition materials that are fired from a weapon

Swimming to survive

German planes fired at the waiting soldiers. The soldiers had nowhere to hide. Fowler knew the best way to escape was to swim. He swam out to a warship. Amazingly, he carried another soldier on his back. When this ship was hit by a bomb, Fowler swam to another boat. This boat took him safely home to England.

France falls to the Germans

In June 1940, the French Prime Minister signed an agreement with Germany. Part of France was allowed to govern itself. The **Nazis** controlled the rest of the country.

German troops parade through the French capital of Paris. They captured the city in June 1940.

Nazis people in the political party that ran Germany from 1933 to 1945

BRITAIN ALONE

Foreign fliers

More than 500 foreign pilots helped the British during the Battle of Britain. They included airmen from Poland, Canada, New Zealand, and the United States.

Germany defeated France in June 1940. Hitler wanted to invade Britain next. But first, he had to weaken the British air force. This meant that the Battle of Britain was fought in the air. Britain had fewer than 700 **fighters**. Germany had 2,600 fighters and **bombers**.

Air battle

On 16 August 1940, **Royal Air Force (RAF)** pilot James Nicholson raced to his fighter. A group of German aircraft was heading toward England.

RAF fighter pilots race to their planes during the Battle of Britain in 1940.

Word Bank   fighter fast aircraft designed to fight and destroy enemy aircraft

Nicholson and two other pilots set off to stop them. An air battle followed. All three RAF planes were hit. Nicholson's plane burst into flames.

Refusal to quit

Nicholson got ready to parachute out of his plane. Just then, he spotted an enemy fighter. The flames began to burn him. But he decided to stay in his plane and fight. He shot down the enemy fighter. Nicholson was badly injured but managed to escape from his plane.

Douglas Bader was a famous English fighter pilot. He lost both his legs in a plane crash. He learned to fly using artificial legs. Bader shot down more than twenty German planes during the Battle of Britain. ➡

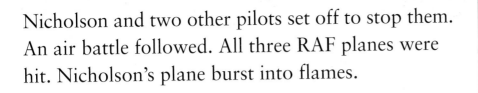

bomber aircraft designed to carry and drop bombs

The Blitz

In August 1940, Winston Churchill ordered **RAF bombers** to attack Berlin, the capital of Germany. This made Hitler very angry. He decided to begin bombing British cities. The British called this bombing "the Blitz".

Constant bombing

The Blitz began in early September 1940. More than 250 German bombers attacked London every night. These **air raids** killed or injured many **civilians**. Thousands of houses and factories were destroyed.

German bombs destroyed many of London's buildings. Luckily, St Paul's Cathedral survived. ➜

Word Bank air raid attack by military aircraft, using bombs or rockets

Invasion is defeated

Between July and December 1940, air raids killed more than 23,000 British civilians. This made the British people even more determined not to let Germany win the war.

Between July and October 1940, RAF fighters destroyed 1,733 German aircraft. The Germans had to give up their plan to invade Britain. The British suffered heavy losses too. The RAF lost more than 900 aircraft and 415 RAF pilots were killed.

Anderson shelters

Thousands of British families built steel shelters (pictured below) in their gardens. These were called Anderson shelters. They helped protect people during German bombing attacks.

civilian someone who is not part of the military

In October 1939, the Germans planned a daring **U-boat** (submarine) attack. Their target was Scapa Flow in Scotland's Orkney Islands. There was a British **naval base** at Scapa Flow. The Germans planned to sink one of the British warships anchored there.

U-47 takes to the sea

Günther Prien was the captain of U-boat U-47. On 8 October, Prien gave the order to head for Scapa Flow. It was a dangerous journey.

Ships sunk

German U-boats sunk huge numbers of **Allied** ships during the war. This table shows how many Allied ships they sunk in each year.

Year		Ships
1939	–	114
1940	–	471
1941	–	432
1942	–	1,160
1943	–	377
1944	–	56
1945	–	55

A torpedo from a U-boat strikes a British cargo ship off the coast of West Africa in 1942.

Word Bank   U-boat German submarine

Direct hit

After more than five days, the submarine finally reached the naval base. U-47 quietly entered the harbour. Then, it fired **torpedoes** at a British **battleship** called the *Royal Oak*. There was a huge explosion. The *Royal Oak* began to sink.

U-47 then escaped from the harbour. It had taken great skill and bravery to carry out the task. Sinking the *Royal Oak* was a huge victory for the Germans.

A German U-boat surfaces in the **English Channel** after attacking Allied ships in the Atlantic Ocean.

torpedo   missile that is fired underwater

Invasion of the Soviet Union

In 1941 Hitler decided to attack the **Soviet Union**, which had not yet joined the **Allies**. The Soviet Union was a **Communist** country. It was rich in materials such as coal and oil. Hitler wanted these materials for Germany. He also hated **Communism**.

In June 1941 German troops and tanks moved into the Soviet Union. The Soviet army was caught by surprise. Large numbers of Soviet troops **surrendered** to the Germans.

Siege of Leningrad

From September 1941 until January 1944, German troops surrounded the Soviet city of Leningrad (now called St Petersburg). The Germans stopped supplies getting into the city. More than 600,000 Soviet people died at Leningrad. Some starved to death. Others were killed by German bombs.

German tanks charge across the Soviet countryside in the summer of 1941.

Word Bank Soviet Union country that once spread across northern Asia and Eastern Europe. It included Russia and other countries.

Huge losses

By the end of September 1941, the Soviets had lost more than two million men. But the Soviet army was still huge.

The big freeze

The Germans were not prepared for the freezing Soviet winter. Their clothes were not warm enough. Their weapons froze. Their vehicles could not move in the snow and mud. Germany's rapid **invasion** came to a halt.

German troops faced freezing temperatures during the Soviet winter of 1941–1942.

THE UNITED STATES JOINS IN

Call to work

During the war, the US government produced posters such as the one below. These posters encouraged women to work in factories that made planes, bombs, and weapons.

Britain was running out of weapons and supplies. But it did not have enough money to pay for more. Winston Churchill asked the United States for help.

Support for an ally

In March 1941, US President Franklin Roosevelt agreed to lend Britain the supplies it needed. These supplies included aircraft, ships, and **ammunition**.

Word Bank   ammunition   materials that are fired from a weapon

The **Soviet Union** also needed aid. Britain and the United States promised to help. Both countries were enemies of **Communism**. But both thought the **Nazis** were a worse enemy.

Trouble in the Far East

In Asia, Roosevelt was worried about Japan. Japan had invaded China three years earlier in 1937. In 1940 Japanese troops moved into Northern Indochina (now called Vietnam). They did this to stop supplies getting to China. This caused the United States to stop trade with Japan.

US factories produced a huge amount of war materials. This factory in Connecticut made more than 6,000 **fighter** planes during the war.

Italy's Benito Mussolini (left) and Germany's Adolf Hitler (right) wanted to control all of Europe.

Nazis people in the political party that ran Germany from 1933 to 1945

Pearl Harbor

On 7 December 1941, US Navy sailor Dorie Miller got up at 6 a.m. He collected the laundry on board a US **battleship**, the *West Virginia*. The ship was at a **naval base** in Pearl Harbor, Hawaii.

Suddenly, an explosion rocked the ship. The *West Virginia* and the other American ships were being attacked. A Japanese **torpedo** had damaged the ship. Miller went up to the deck.

Surprise attack!

The Japanese attack on Pearl Harbor surprised the US Navy. The attack lasted two hours. Japanese planes sunk or damaged eighteen US ships. They also destroyed 170 US planes. The attack killed 2,403 Americans.

This photo shows Japanese **dive-bombers** getting ready to attack Pearl Harbor.

Word Bank   battleship   large warship carrying big guns

Right man for the job

Fire burned everywhere. Even the water in the harbour was in flames. Miller carried the ship's injured captain to a safer part of the ship.

Miller was the ship's cook. He had not been trained to use a machine gun. But he decided to start shooting at the Japanese planes. The burning ship was sinking fast. Miller kept firing the machine gun until he was told to **abandon ship**.

The USS *Arizona* was also sunk at Pearl Harbor. It took less than nine minutes to sink. More than 1,100 of its crew died.

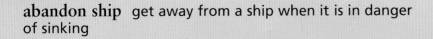

abandon ship   get away from a ship when it is in danger of sinking

WAR IN THE PACIFIC

After the attack on Pearl Harbor, the United States and Britain declared war on Japan. Germany and Italy were on the same side as Japan. So they declared war on the United States.

Japanese advance

In December 1942, the Japanese sunk two British warships near Malaya. They also captured the British **colony** of Hong Kong. Two months later, they captured Singapore. Singapore was a major British **naval base**.

Doolittle Raid

The photo below shows an American **bomber** setting off for a bombing raid on Japan. US pilot Jimmy Doolittle led the raid on 18 April 1942. The Doolittle Raid did not do much damage. But it did prove it was possible to attack Japan.

After the Pearl Harbor attack, Japan quickly captured other areas in the Pacific.

SOVIET UNION
(also known as the USSR)

N
W   E
S

MONGOLIA

Beijing

CHINA

KOREA

JAPAN

Hiroshima

Tokyo

Nagasaki

Okinawa

INDIA

Iwo Jima

BURMA

Hong Kong

INDOCHINA

Mariana Is.

SIAM (Thailand)

Bataan

Guam

PHILIPPINES   Battle of Leyte Gulf

MALAYA

Singapore

DUTCH EAST INDIES

Java Sea

INDIAN OCEAN

Darwin

Coral Sea

AUSTRALIA

PACIFIC OCEAN

USA

0   3000 km
0   2000 miles

Battle of Midway
Midway Is.

Pearl Harbor

Marshall Is.

Hawaiian Is.

Tarawa   Gilbert Is.

Guadalcanal

Key
Major battle or air attack

Word Bank   colony overseas territory that has been taken over and run by a foreign country

The United States is defeated

The Japanese also attacked the Philippines. This was an American colony. On 9 April 1942, US and Filipino troops in the Philippines **surrendered**.

Death march

The Japanese treated **POWs (prisoners of war)** very badly. They forced the captured Americans to march to **prison camps**. About 5,200 US soldiers died on the march. It became known as the Bataan Death March.

These are some of the US troops captured in the Philippines. They took part in the Bataan Death March.

prison camp   place where people were forced to live and work

Guadalcanal

In July 1942, the Japanese began to build an airfield in the South Pacific. This airfield was on the island of Guadalcanal (see map on page 22).

US marines captured the airfield. Sergeant Mitchell Paige and his **battalion** were sent to defend it. Paige set up four machine guns. On 26 October 1942, Japanese troops attacked.

The Japanese attack

The Japanese attacked at night. By dawn, Paige was the only one in his unit still able to fight.

Two US marines take aim during the Battle of Guadalcanal in 1942. They are firing a machine gun at Japanese planes.

Word Bank   aircraft carrier huge ship with a flat deck. The deck acts as a runway for naval planes.

A lone stand

Paige wanted the Japanese to think there were lots of men still fighting. He ran around, firing the different machine guns. Then he picked up a machine gun and ran. He kept on firing the heavy gun. Enemy soldiers fell dead all around him.

Before long, the Japanese troops **retreated**. The Japanese never recaptured the airfield.

These are Japanese soldiers on Guadalcanal. They are firing a machine gun at US troops.

retreat   move back

THE ALLIES TURN THE TIDE

In 1940 Italy invaded Egypt. They wanted to control the Suez Canal in Egypt, Africa. If they did this, they could stop **Allied** supplies getting to the **Far East**.

British forces fought back. They forced the Italians out of Egypt. Then the Germans joined the fight. German troops were led by Erwin Rommel.

Battle of El Alamein

In 1942, Allied troops fought the Germans in El Alamein, Egypt. General Bernard Montgomery led the **Allies**. The battle lasted twelve days.

The Desert Fox

Erwin Rommel (below left) was one of the **Nazis'** most brilliant soldiers. He was known as "the Desert Fox". This was because he was cunning. It was hard to guess what he would do next.

Australian soldiers during the Battle of El Alamein. They are with a wounded German prisoner. ➔

Word Bank Far East countries of east and southeast Asia. These include China, Japan, Vietnam, the Philippines, Malaysia, and Singapore.

Allied troops pushed the German army out of Egypt. El Alamein was an important victory for the Allies.

Operation Torch

A few days later, the Allies began Operation Torch. US troops landed in North Africa. They came to join Montgomery's forces and crush Rommel's army.

By May 1943, Allied forces had taken 200,000 prisoners. The Allies now controlled North Africa.

The Allies had many more tanks than the Germans at El Alamein. This helped the Allies win the battle.

Battle of Stalingrad

On 19 August 1942, German forces attacked the city of Stalingrad. Stalingrad (now called Volgograd) was an important Soviet city.

A long battle followed. The two sides fought over every house and every street. The Soviets finally defeated the Germans on 2 February 1943.

Hours of waiting

Vassili Zaitsev was a Soviet **sniper** in Stalingrad. His task was to kill as many **Nazi** officers as possible.

Soviet pride

Soviet workers played a very important part in the war. Many worked twelve hours every day in factories. This meant the Soviets produced war materials faster than anyone else.

Soviet troops patrol Stalingrad. They are moving past a burnt-out German tank.

Word Bank   sniper   hidden soldier who shoots enemy soldiers. Snipers shoot from long distances with a special gun.

Zaitsev and his partner waited for hours in their hiding place. Eventually, three German officers and a German sniper appeared. Within seconds the four Nazis lay dead.

Patience pays off

In return, the Germans fired at the snipers with **artillery**. The Soviets then knew where the Germans were hiding. They killed them all. The Soviets also knew where the artillery was hidden. It was no longer safe for the Germans to use these guns in daylight.

Bloodiest battle

The Battle of Stalingrad was the bloodiest battle in history. More than a million Soviet soldiers died. There were 300,000 Germans at Stalingrad. Only 91,000 survived.

German **POWs** walk away from the ruins of Stalingrad in February 1943.

artillery large guns that fire shells or missiles

Invasion of Sicily

The **Allies** had captured North Africa. Their next target was the Italian island of Sicily.

On 10 July 1943 **Allied** troops arrived at Sicily. The Germans fought hard. But the Allies captured the island in mid-August. They also reached the Italian mainland.

US troops scramble up a hill during a battle in Italy in 1943.

Word Bank   monastery building where monks live and pray

The end of Mussolini

After the capture of Sicily, many Italians did not want to carry on fighting. Italy's leader was Benito Mussolini. He was forced to step down in July 1943.

Italy's new prime minister made peace with the Allies. Then Italy joined the Allies and declared war on Germany.

Hitler rushed German troops into Italy. Terrible battles followed. On 4 June 1944, Allied troops freed Rome, the Italian capital.

Monte Cassino

In February 1944, the Allies made a hard decision. They decided to bomb the historic **monastery** at Monte Cassino, near Rome. The Allies believed Germans were hiding there. The bombs destroyed almost everything.

British troops are welcomed in northern Italy in 1945.

The **Allies** invaded France on 6 June 1944. The **invasion** was called D-Day (see also pages 4–5). It was the largest invasion by sea in history.

Fake invasion

The Allies tricked the Germans. They made the Germans think they were going to invade north-east France. The Allies sent false radio messages about their plans. They also made fake tanks and

US troops arrive in Normandy on D-Day.

Word Bank   English Channel   narrow part of the Atlantic Ocean that separates Britain from France

ships. These looked real from the air. Hitler moved thousands of troops to north-east France.

But the Allies did not invade north-east France. Instead, they invaded Normandy in the west. US, Canadian, and British troops took part in the invasion. They crossed the **English Channel** and landed at five beaches in Normandy.

Paratroopers

About 13,000 **paratroopers** also took part in the Normandy invasion. They landed the night before D-Day. Each paratrooper carried a rifle, a compass, medical kit, chocolate bars, and chewing gum.

US paratroopers drop into France as part of the Normandy invasion.

paratrooper soldier that drops into battle using a parachute

Battle of the Bulge

After D-Day, the **Allied** troops moved through France. Hitler made a last attempt to win the war.

In December 1944, the Germans attacked the **Allies** in the Ardennes region of Belgium. People called this the Battle of the Bulge.

Surrounded

Darrell Powers was a US **paratrooper** in the Battle of the Bulge. He and the other men in his company were in some woods. They were surrounded by German troops.

US troops fought in freezing weather during the Battle of the Bulge.

Word Bank   POW (prisoner of war)   prisoner who is captured by the enemy during a war

Good eyesight

Suddenly, Powers noticed something odd. He saw a tree that had not been there the day before. His sergeant checked the spot.

The Germans were moving **artillery** among the trees. They were using the tree to hide the artillery. The Americans fired and the Germans left the spot.

Powers' sharp eyesight saved other American lives later in the battle. It helped him find and kill German **snipers**.

German defeat

The Battle of the Bulge caught the Allies by surprise. The Germans captured more than 21,000 Allied troops. But the battle ended in defeat for the Germans.

A German tank passes a line of American **POWs**. This picture was taken in the first days of the Battle of the Bulge.

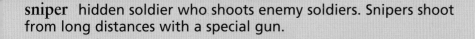

sniper hidden soldier who shoots enemy soldiers. Snipers shoot from long distances with a special gun.

Allies advance

After winning the Battle of the Bulge, the **Allies** pushed on. Soon, only the River Rhine separated the Allies from the centre of Germany. Hitler ordered all bridges across the Rhine to be destroyed.

Bridge to victory

Incredibly, US troops found one bridge still standing. This bridge was in the town of Remagen. Thousands of US troops crossed over this bridge.

Dresden bombing

The German city of Dresden (pictured below) was famous for its beauty. But in February 1945, **Allied** bombs destroyed Dresden. About 100,000 German **civilians** died in the attack. Some people thought the bombing was unnecessary.

Word Bank   civilian someone who is not part of the military

Allies meet in Germany

Meanwhile, the Soviet Army moved into Germany from the east. On 25 April 1945, the Russian and American armies met up for the first time. They met at Torgau, Germany.

Hitler dies

On 30 April 1945, Hitler killed himself. One week later, Germany **surrendered** to the Allies. People around the world celebrated VE (Victory in Europe) Day.

Soldiers fly the Soviet flag over Berlin. The Soviets captured Berlin in May 1945.

THE FALL OF JAPAN

The **Allies** had won the war in Europe. They were still fighting the war in the Pacific. American troops moved from one Pacific island to the next. Each island took them closer to Japan.

Return to the Philippines

The United States needed to recapture the Philippines. General Douglas MacArthur led more than 150,000 troops into battle. He also brought 700 ships.

General MacArthur arrives back at Leyte Island in the Philippines in October 1944. He had been forced to leave the island in 1942. But he had promised to return.

The Battle of Leyte Gulf followed. It was a huge sea battle. American warships and planes destroyed most of the Japanese fleet.

Final land battles

The United States needed to capture the islands of Iwo Jima and Okinawa. Then they could launch aircraft from these islands to bomb Japan.

Both battles were fought on land. The Americans won, but the battles were long. Thousands died.

Kamikazes

Kamikaze aircraft were Japanese planes loaded with explosives. A kamikaze pilot would fly his plane into its target knowing he would die in the attack. Kamikaze planes were used for the first time at the Battle of Leyte Gulf. They were used to attack **Allied** warships.

US marines raise the American flag on Iwo Jima.

The A-bomb

While US troops captured Pacific islands, US **bombers** attacked Japanese cities. In March 1945, they bombed Tokyo. The bombing killed more than 100,000 people and destroyed huge areas of the city.

Fighting to death

But these terrible attacks did not make the Japanese give up. If the United States invaded Japan, many more soldiers would die. The United States wanted a quicker end to the war.

Guns on a US **aircraft carrier** fire at Japanese **fighters**.

Word Bank   atomic bomb extremely destructive bomb powered by the release of nuclear energy

The atomic bombs

On 6 August 1945, Colonel Paul Tibbets set off on a mission. His bomber was named the *Enola Gay*. Just after 8 a.m., the *Enola Gay* dropped the first **atomic bomb** over the city of Hiroshima, Japan. The atomic bomb was a nuclear weapon of mass destruction. In a flash, most of the city was wiped out.

Three days later, the United States dropped a second atomic bomb on Nagasaki, Japan. On 2 September 1945, Japan surrendered. The war was over.

Ball of fire

When the atomic bombs dropped on Hiroshima and Nagasaki, a huge mushroom-shaped cloud (like the one pictured below) appeared over the cities. The results were horrific. Many died immediately. Other people died more slowly and more painfully.

These girls are in Hiroshima after the atomic bomb. They are wearing masks to block the smell of dead bodies.

TIMELINE

1939

1 September   Germany invades Poland.

3 September   Britain, France, New Zealand, Australia, and India declare war on Germany.

10 September Canada declares war on Germany.

1940

9 April   Germany invades Denmark and Norway.

10–13 May   Germany invades Luxembourg, Belgium, the Netherlands, and France.

26 May   The rescue of British, French, and Belgian troops from the beaches of Dunkirk begins.

10 June   Italy declares war on France and Britain.

22 June   France **surrenders** to Germany.

10 July   The Battle of Britain begins.

7 September   The Blitz begins, as Germany drops bombs on London and other British cities.

27 September Japan, Germany, and Italy agree to work together.

1941

22 June   Germany invades the **Soviet Union**.

7 December   Japan attacks the US **naval base** at Pearl Harbor.

8 December   The United States and Britain declare war on Japan.

11 December   Germany and Italy declare war on the United States.

1942

18 April   Jimmy Doolittle leads a daring bombing raid on Japan.

4–6 June   Japan is defeated in the Battle of Midway.

7 August   US Marines capture the Japanese airfield on Guadalcanal.

23 October	General Bernard Montgomery leads **Allied** troops into the Battle of El Alamein.
4 November	Rommel and his troops **retreat** from El Alamein.
8 November	The Allied **invasion** of North Africa, named Operation Torch, begins.

1943

2 February	The Germans surrender to the Soviet Army at Stalingrad.
10 July	The **Allies** land on Sicily, Italy.
25 July	Benito Mussolini is forced out as leader of Italy.
3 September	Italy surrenders to the Allies.

1944

27 January	The Soviets defeat the Germans at Leningrad.
4 June	Rome falls to the Allies.
6 June	The Allies launch a massive invasion of Normandy (D-Day).
23–26 October	US victory at the Battle of Leyte Gulf.
16 December	The Battle of the Bulge begins.

1945

17 January	Soviet troops capture Warsaw, Poland.
19 February	American troops invade Iwo Jima.
1 April	American soldiers land at Okinawa.
22 April	Soviet troops surround Berlin.
30 April	Adolf Hitler kills himself.
8 May	People around the world celebrate VE Day.
6 August	The United States drops an **atomic bomb** on Hiroshima, Japan.
9 August	A second atomic bomb is dropped on Nagasaki, Japan.
2 September	Japan surrenders.

FIND OUT MORE

Websites

BBC History
This BBC website is a good, all-round site for the study of World War II.
http://www.bbc.co.uk/dna/ww2

Eyewitness to History
The "World War II" section of this website is full of eyewitness accounts of key events of the war.
http://www.eyewitnesstohistory.com/w2frm.htm

Britannica
This Britannica site gives a step-by-step account of the Normandy landings. It has interactive charts and maps, audio recordings, and old newsreels.
http://www.britannica.com/dday

Books

The Battle of Britain, by Alex Woolf (Hodder Wayland, 2003)

The Second World War, by Reg Grant (Franklin Watts, 2005)

The Second World War, by Stewart Ross (Evans, 2003)

DVD/VHS

Films about World War II are often aimed at an adult audience. Ask a parent or teacher before watching these.

The World at War 30th Anniversary Edition (DVD 2004)
A visual history of World War II.

Tora! Tora! Tora! (1970)
A story about the Pearl Harbor attack told from both the American and Japanese points of view.

Band of Brothers (2001)
A ten-part story that follows a company of US paratroopers from D-Day to the end of the war.

World wide web

To find out more about World War II you can search the Internet. Use keywords such as these:

- "Pacific war"
- World War II + North Africa
- World War II + Blitz

You can find your own keywords by using words from this book. The search tips below will help you find useful websites.

Most sites are aimed at adults. They can contain upsetting information and pictures. Make sure that you use well-known sites with correct information, such as those listed on page 44.

Search tips

There are billions of pages on the Internet. It can be difficult to find exactly what you are looking for. These tips will help you find useful websites more quickly:

- Know what you want to find out about.
- Use simple keywords.
- Use two to six keywords in a search.
- Only use names of people, places, or things.
- Put double quote marks around words that go together, for example "Operation Torch".

Where to search

Search engine
A search engine looks through millions of website pages. It lists all the sites that match the words in the search box. You will find the best matches are at the top of the list, on the first page.

Search directory
A person instead of a computer has sorted a search directory. You can search by keyword or subject and browse through the different sites. It is like looking through books on a library shelf.

abandon ship get away from a ship when it is in danger of sinking

air raid attack by military aircraft, using bombs or rockets

aircraft carrier huge ship with a flat deck. The deck acts as a runway for naval planes.

Allied belonging to the group of nations that fought against Germany, Italy, and Japan

Allies group of nations that fought against Germany, Italy, and Japan in World War II

ammunition materials that are fired from a weapon

artillery large guns that fire shells or missiles

atomic bomb extremely destructive bomb powered by the release of nuclear energy

battalion large military unit made up of 200 to 1,000 troops

battleship large warship carrying big guns

bomber aircraft designed to carry and drop bombs

civilian someone who is not part of the military

colony overseas territory that has been taken over and run by a foreign country

Communism one-party system of government that puts equality above freedom

Communist someone who supports Communism, a one-party system of government

dive-bomber plane that dives down towards its target before dropping its explosives

English Channel narrow part of the Atlantic Ocean that separates Britain from France

Far East countries of east and southeast Asia. These include China, Japan, Vietnam, the Philippines, Malaysia, and Singapore.

fighter fast aircraft designed to fight and destroy enemy aircraft

howitzer cannon on wheels that is pulled into place by a tractor or jeep

invasion entry by armed forces into a territory, often to conquer that territory

monastery building where monks live and pray

naval base place where a navy's ships are harboured and maintained

Nazis people in the political party that ran Germany from 1933 to 1945

paratrooper soldier that drops into battle using a parachute

POW (prisoner of war) prisoner who is captured and put in prison by the enemy during a war

prison camp place where people were forced to live and work

retreat move back

Royal Air Force (RAF) British air force

sniper hidden soldier who shoots enemy soldiers. Snipers shoot from long distances with a special gun.

Soviet Union country that once spread across northern Asia and Eastern Europe. It included Russia and other countries.

surrender give yourself up to the enemy

torpedo missile that is fired underwater

U-boat German submarine

INDEX